Eleanor 

&

Mary McLeod Bethune:

An Unusual Friendship

Camesha Whittaker, Ph.D.

Foreword by

Dr. Nido Qubein

Award Winning Author &

President of High Point University

Illustrated by

R.J. Rosasco

Eleanor Roosevelt & Mary McLeod Bethune:
An Unusual Friendship
by
Camesha Whittaker, Ph.D.

For permissions contact:
ace@advancecivility.com
Published by

Advance Civility Press, LLC
1500 Beville Road, Suite 606-321
Daytona Beach, FL 32114
www.advancecivilitypress.com

For book and author inquiries visit
www.rooseveltandbethune.com

Library of Congress Control Number: 2021925556
ISBN: 978-0-578-30137-2
Printed in the United States of America

DEDICATION

To my children,
Asha-Mahri and MJ.

To young people everywhere who deserve
equal opportunity and pathways to achieve
their most innovative aspirations.

For everyone who, like Mary McLeod Bethune and Eleanor
Roosevelt, is committed to affecting transformation in their
corner of the earth.

To the empowerment of youth, mobilization of women, and
the improvement of interracial relationships.

To the advancement of civility worldwide!

CONTENTS

FOREWORD BY DR. NIDO QUBEIN

This is a provocatively interesting work by an accomplished and respected author.

You'll love reading the historical chronicle of two women who, in their own ways, helped to change history. Dr. Camesha Whittaker weaves the reporting on the relationship between Roosevelt and Bethune in an interesting, inspiring, and engaging manner. You'll benefit measurably from the insights and conclusions of the author and become more convinced that civility and inclusion are possible realities for us all. Dr. Whittaker's style is friendly yet direct. Her purpose for writing this narrative is both important and instructive.

I've admired Dr. Whittaker as an educator and a community leader. Her stewardship at Bethune-Cookman University is respected and celebrated. Her communication skills connect with people from all walks of life and her commitment to building relational capital is admired and appreciated.

In these times of "too much information" and "not enough understanding" Dr. Whittaker's literary contribution makes a big difference for all those who want to remain or become responsible citizens and caring friends of humanity. Read this book to learn, to study, and to share with others.

PREFACE

It has been twenty-five years since I first heard Mary McLeod Bethune and Eleanor Roosevelt mentioned in the same sentence. As a new international student at Bethune-Cookman College, I participated in a campus tour during freshman orientation. As the guide walked our cohort through the Mary McLeod Bethune Foundation, she mentioned that the two women were friends and that the First Lady visited with Mrs. Bethune at her home. I was in awe, and wanted to know more about this seemingly unusual friendship.

On February 10, 2000, a few months before completing my undergraduate degree, the Daytona Beach News-Journal ran a feature story in the Neighbors' section. The headline read, "Students, colleagues and friends of B-CC founder Mary McLeod Bethune say her kindness, influence and wisdom will never be forgotten. They hope to...STAY THE COURSE...and make a better world for themselves and others."

The left side of the Black History Month article featured a photograph of Eleanor Roosevelt presenting an honorary doctorate to Mary McLeod Bethune. The right side of the page was anchored with a photograph of me talking with a student in front of the college's main administrative building. That caption read, "B-CC Student Government President Camesha Whittaker, left, enjoys a day on campus with fellow student ...Whittaker says students should not take for granted the accomplishment of the college's founder." These words that I spoke 21 years ago resonated with me. In 2005 when I began my Ph.D. studies, there was no question that my research would include Mary McLeod Bethune and Eleanor Roosevelt. These transformative figures had inspired my commitment to global citizenship, education, and communication, and my desire to create solutions to advance people and organizations.

Since no one had identified the nature and impact of their friendship, I decided to conduct a historiographical study to examine their interpersonal communication. As part of the study, my primary research analyzed more than 800 pieces of correspondence archived at the Franklin Delano Roosevelt Library in Hyde Park, NY, and examined historical documents from The Mary McLeod Bethune Papers: The Bethune-Cookman College Collection, 1922 - 1955.

My primary research included in-depth interviews with Mr. James Huger in 2007 and Dr. Dorothy I. Height in 2008. They were two individuals who shared their personal experiences regarding the two women's friendship. Huger was Bethune's former student and employee who was selected to represent her in various public service capacities during the course of her relationship with Mrs. Roosevelt. Height was the former Chair and President Emerita of the National Council of Negro Women (NCNW), an organization founded by Bethune and strongly supported by Eleanor Roosevelt. She worked on projects both women gave her and observed their friendship up closely. My interview with Dr. Height was held at the NCNW national headquarters in July 2008. Dr. Height died on April 20, 2010, at the age of 98.

It has been over a decade since I published the doctoral dissertation about Roosevelt and Bethune. However, what remained unsettling for me was the reality the message about their friendship and its impact on the world would not be read by most people, particularly young adults. It became important to present as much of their work that is centered on leaving a legacy for young people. Their impact on women's rights, education, civil rights, and human rights provides a model for how relationships can be utilized for a purpose much greater than self. Both women saw interracial cooperation as a way to improve a nation. It is my hope that this message will be an inspiration to all readers.

Writing about the relationship between two of the most powerful women in America during the 20th Century was not simply a way to disseminate historical facts. I wrote about this important relationship so that all can learn more about their significant global impact and the legacy of civility. This is the reason the end of this book features "A Pledge to Civility as a Citizen of the World (Inspired by the impactful friendship between Eleanor Roosevelt & Mary McLeod Bethune)." We, too, can impact our corner of the earth by committing to building intentional, respectful and meaningful relationships at home, in schools, in churches, civic organizations, and in the global marketplace.

ACKNOWLEDGMENTS

I have had the extraordinary blessing of companions on the journey who have contributed to my overall development from childhood to adulthood. I am thankful to each of you, for your presence and demonstration of commitment to my work, service, and calling.

This project was God-inspired and personally supported by family members and close friends who shared the belief that the relationship between Mary McLeod Bethune and Eleanor Roosevelt needed to be told beyond the pages of my published dissertation.

To my mother, Patricia Williams Daley, thank you for your unconditional love, the gift of education, and your constant encouragement. Pop Daley, your love and candid feedback have been invaluable.

Special thanks to friends whose support and understanding enhanced this work: Dr. Estrelda Alexander, Miss Gaihovanie Bonami, Dr. Mary Buck, Mrs. Fay Gayle (editor), and Mrs. Yassah Lee. To Pastor Derrick G. Jackson, thank you for your prayers and your constant reassurance throughout this journey.

To my daughter, Asha-Mahri, your insight into this manuscript was refreshing and energetic and just what I needed.

To Dalma, your love and personal commitment to this project made it possible for me to share it with the world. Thank you for always sharing the vision for innovation and impact.

1

Illustration depicting Eleanor Roosevelt and Mary McLeod Bethune writing letters

"Lots of love to a friend who
has proven to be a friend."
(Mary McLeod Bethune, 1949)

"Perhaps my first really close friendship with a
Negro of about my own age started with a woman
who is now a dear friend:
Mrs. Mary McLeod Bethune."
(Eleanor Roosevelt, 1953)

CHAPTER 1
Background and Introduction

Although acts of incivility and racial intolerance are widely publicized by the media, it is not strange to observe friendships among individuals from different racial backgrounds in modern-day America. However, Mary McLeod Bethune and Eleanor Roosevelt's friendship began in the early twentieth century, when racial violence was common, and many considered their friendship quite uncommon.

Imagine a white First Lady of the United States and a black civil rights leader and educator becoming friends at a time when the country was deeply divided by race and intense discrimination. Cross-racial relationships were rare in the 1930s. Blacks and whites were not known to have civil exchanges or close friendships, and, certainly, there were no publicized examples of such relationships between national figures.

Roosevelt and Bethune broke the social norms as historical figures, who rose to prominence during times of racial conflict in the United States. They became friends and worked to unify the races, advanced the causes of those who were being marginalized, and brought hope for people suffering from the enduring effects of discrimination and racism.

Many historians and researchers have studied their individual lives. Some authors have published biographies about their roles as leaders, educators, and human rights activists. A few have told stories about Eleanor Roosevelt and her white friends, but there is no published book that explores the nature of her relationship with Mary McLeod Bethune.

Several articles and historical organizations acknowledge their friendship, but only one dissertation takes a closer look at their relationship. This book is based on the author's published dissertation entitled "Eleanor Roosevelt and Mary McLeod Bethune: An Unusual Friendship during Uncommon Times and its Continued Contribution to Social Change."

What did Mary McLeod Bethune, a daughter of former slaves and founder of a Historically Black College and University (HBCU) in the 20th Century, have in common with a First Lady of the United States who was born into a privileged, wealthy family? They shared a commitment to improving the lives of those who were most in need. Learning about the relationship of these historical, political figures and societal leaders will serve as an example of how friendships and relationships with people from different backgrounds can lead to personal and community progress.

In this book, you will read about the life stories of the "First Lady of The Struggle–Mary McLeod Bethune" and the "First Lady of the World–Eleanor Roosevelt." You will explore the historical conditions that surrounded their friendship, examine their communication throughout the decades, and discover how their relationship impacted their work with the National Youth Administration, Bethune-Cookman College (now University), and the National Council of Negro Women.

Finally, you will understand how Mrs. Roosevelt and Mrs. Bethune's uncommon friendship during uncommon times contributed to advancing social change in the United States and how it still serves as a model for how civility can be achieved and practiced amidst differences in our global society.

Illustration depicting Mary McLeod Bethune in front of The Mary McLeod Bethune Foundation

2

Illustration depicting Mary McLeod Bethune's childhood home in Mayesville, SC

CHAPTER 2
Meet the First Lady of the Struggle: Mary McLeod Bethune

Born on July 10, 1875, in a log cabin near Mayesville, South Carolina, Mary Jane McLeod was the fifteenth child and the first of her seventeen siblings not born into slavery. Her parents, Samuel and Patsy McIntosh McLeod, were former slaves on the McIntosh and McLeod plantations. When her mother realized she still owed her slave owner, she continued to work on the plantation to work off the debt. Eventually, she saved enough money to buy the cabin where Mary Jane McLeod was born.

Although Mary Jane McLeod was born 14 years after the American Civil War (1861-1865), the effects of the war profoundly influenced her life. Known as the first battle on U.S. soil, this four-year conflict arose because northern states and southern states disagreed about whether slavery was morally right or wrong. The northern states believed slavery was a threat to their economic and social progress, while, the southern states depended on the system of slavery to support their economy. As a result, eleven southern states separated from the rest of the country and formed the Confederacy.

The southern states elected Jefferson Davis to lead them into battle. The northern states and federal government were under the leadership of Abraham Lincoln, the sixteenth President of the United States. Lincoln considered slavery unjust and strongly opposed its expansion. The war claimed the lives of 600,000 Americans and ended with the defeat of the Confederate States. On January 1, 1863, Lincoln signed the landmark executive orders for the Emancipation Proclamation that declared the freedom of slaves within the Confederate States.

The close of the Civil War and the signing of the Emancipation Proclamation marked the end of slavery. But, when Mary Jane McLeod entered the world in 1875, the country was still rebuilding due to the devastating effects of the war. She was born free, but her life in a racially segregated society was not without struggle. Nevertheless, her parents were committed to making a better life for the family. Their children worked on the slave plantation, and by the time Mary Jane McLeod was nine years old, she could pick at least two hundred pounds of cotton in one day.

McLeod's first exposure to formal education began at age ten when she was enrolled at a school started by the Mission Board of the Presbyterian Church. She was the only one in her family to attend school. Though she walked several miles to and from school daily, she was eager to return home to share her new knowledge with her family.

Undoubtedly, Mary's passion for missionary work, education, and the advancement of women's issues became a part of her life's goals from a very early age. Consequently, she dedicated herself to formal academic preparation to qualify her for the vocation. Upon completing training at Trinity Presbyterian School in Mayesville, SC in 1887, Mary Jane McLeod received a scholarship to pursue the Normal and Scientific Course of Scotia Seminary in Concord, NC. She graduated in 1894 after six years of instruction. A year later, she completed training from The Bible School for Home and Foreign Mission in Chicago (known today as the Moody Bible Institute). At that time, Mary Jane McLeod was the only black student to attend the school.

Determined to help those most in need, McLeod wanted to do missionary work in Africa. However, her application to the Mission Board of the Presbyterian Church for a missionary assignment in Africa went unfulfilled. Alternatively, she dedicated herself to working with local missions and returned to the Mayesville Presbyterian Mission School to assist her former teacher, Miss Wilson. Later, Mary Jane McLeod taught for Haines Institute (Atlanta, GA) and the Kindell Institute in Sumter, South Carolina.

In 1898 Mary Jane McLeod married Albertus Bethune. A year later, she gave birth to their only biological son, Albert Bethune. Mary McLeod Bethune now began to immerse herself in a life dedicated to serving others. In 1899, the Bethune family relocated to Palatka, Florida, to lead a Presbyterian Mission School. While there, Bethune provided outreach to prisoners and tried to help those believed to be innocent. Upon learning of the railroad project in Daytona Beach that would attract black families looking for work in the area, Bethune felt a burning desire to build a school to help young girls that would improve their role in the home and the workforce. Despite her husband's lack of support for what he considered big, lofty goals, she never gave up on her dream. On October 3, 1904, Bethune founded the Daytona Normal and Industrial School for Negro Girls (now Bethune-Cookman University, Daytona Beach, FL) on what was previously a city garbage dump.

Historians comment on Bethune's determination and courage that allowed her to found Bethune-Cookman College by noting that she did it with faith in God, five little girls, and a $1.50. But, Bethune had so much more. By the time she arrived in Daytona Beach, she had experienced poverty, racism, grief, loss, and denial, but she also had a vision for equality and a strategic plan to enlist support from unlikely but capable benefactors in unfamiliar places. She baked and sold sweet potato pies, solicited financial help from many, including the son of James Gamble (1803-1891), co-founder of Proctor & Gamble, whom she convinced to serve on the institution's Board of Trustees. In sum, Mary McLeod Bethune combined her Christian faith with her communication, teaching, advocacy, fundraising, and entrepreneurial skills. With her knowledge and experience, she innovated an educational oasis for black people who were excluded from opportunities in a country they helped to build.

In addition to her commitment to education, Mary McLeod Bethune became involved in civic and community affairs. As a leader of several organizations, including the Southeastern Federation of Colored Women's Clubs (1920-1925) and the National Association of Teachers in Colored Schools (1923-1924), Bethune exercised her belief in the power of organizing people around a central cause. She believed that the best way to improve conditions for Blacks at home and abroad was to combine the group's efforts towards influencing political decisions that often determined the standard of living for Black people. This kind of vision is one of the reasons she founded the National Council of Negro Women in 1935.

A victim of racism and sexism from an early age, Bethune advocated for educational, racial, and social justice. Yet this founder of the

National Council of Negro Women, organizer of the United Negro College Fund, and columnist for the Chicago Defender was not only concerned about social injustices in the United States. Her travel as a consultant, U.S. ambassador, and a special international guest to Italy, Switzerland, Germany, Holland, Belgium, France, and Scotland enlarged her worldview. Further, the global community validated her contributions to civil rights and women's rights. Countries such as the Republic of Haiti and Liberia were among those that bestowed upon her humanitarian awards.

As an activist, Bethune's speeches and published articles influenced diverse audiences and challenged existing societal standards. Beginning in the 1920s, she wrote several letters to the White House requesting changes in public policy that affected the equality of all people. Because of her influence, Bethune gained access to four U.S. Presidents (Calvin Coolidge, Herbert Hoover, Franklin Delano Roosevelt, and Harry S. Truman) and First Lady Eleanor Roosevelt. She was the first Black person appointed as a ranking specialist in the National Youth Administration (NYA), a New Deal agency established in 1935 by Franklin Delano Roosevelt as part of the Works Progress Administration (WPA). It provided job training to young people facing unemployment because of the Depression. Bethune directed Negro Affairs for the NYA from 1936 to 1944. And while she lobbied for the U.S. government to eliminate practices discriminating against blacks, she did not neglect global issues or war-related concerns.

Bethune also used her platform to address issues of social change. She delivered several speeches to the U.S. Congress, the National Council of Negro Women, and the National Youth Administration and gave various public addresses, including the 1942 radio address, during the middle of World War II, in which she responded to the question "What are we Fighting For?" To energize support among Blacks Bethune said,

> ...These are the days for a united front with a united purpose to fight for that victory which we must have, or, regardless of caste, creed or position, we will all sink together.
> What are we fighting for? We are fighting for the perfection of the democracy of our own beloved America, and the extension of that perfected democracy to the ends of the world.

Although Bethune retired from Bethune-Cookman in 1947 and from the National Council of Negro Women in 1949, in a 1955 Chicago Defender article, she emphasized that she was "forever rallying the general citizenry in support of noble causes." In 1974, a statue of Bethune was erected directly across from Abraham Lincoln's statue in Washington, DC's Lincoln Park. In February 2022, another statue of Bethune will be installed in the United States Capitol Rotunda replacing the nearly century-old statue of Confederate General Edmund Kirby Smith.

Illustration depicting a statue of Dr. Mary McLeod Bethune on the campus of Bethune-Cookman University

Illustration depicting First Lady Eleanor Roosevelt speaking at a national press conference

Illustration depicting Eleanor Roosevelt's childhood home in Germantown, NY

CHAPTER 3
Meet the First Lady of the World: Anna Eleanor Roosevelt

Harry Truman, the 33rd President of the United States, gave Anna Eleanor Roosevelt the title "First Lady of the World." He recognized her lifelong contributions to civil and human rights. As a result, in 1945, he invited her to join the first United States delegation to the United Nations.

Anna Eleanor Roosevelt was born on October 11, 1884, in New York City, but preferred to be called Eleanor instead of Anna. Although she was born into an influential and wealthy family, her life had challenges. Eleanor Roosevelt was orphaned at ten years old. Her mother, Anna Hall, of the wealthy Livingston family of New York, died in 1892 when Eleanor was eight years old. Her father, Elliot Roosevelt (brother of the 26th United States President Theodore Roosevelt), died in 1894 due to alcohol addiction. Eleanor had one half-brother; she was the only girl and oldest of three children born to both parents. After her parents passed away, her grandmother, Mary Livingston Ludlow Hall, became her legal guardian. Anna Hall did not consider her only daughter physically beautiful and nicknamed her "granny." Apart from losing both parents, her mother's perception contributed to Eleanor's struggle with low self-esteem.

Yet, Eleanor's grandmother supported her educational development. Her decisions on Eleanor's educational journey impacted her path in life. She received private tutoring for several years before being sent to Allenswood, an exclusive boarding school for girls outside London,

England, from age 15 to 18. These experiences helped to form her perspective about women's empowerment and transformation. Under the tutelage and mentorship of the school's headmistress, Mademoiselle Marie Souvestre, Eleanor began developing her self-confidence and a passion for helping transform women's lives.

In 1903, when Eleanor Roosevelt returned to the United States, she began pursuing a life of service by helping people who were most in need. Her study in England developed her interest in assisting women in thinking more about themselves although she thought little about herself. Consequently, Eleanor became involved in social service work. She joined the Junior League, a service organization for women, and took on her first teaching assignment at the Rivington Street Settlement House.

Eleanor became engaged to her distant cousin, Franklin Delano Roosevelt, in 1903. They married in 1905 and had six children in ten years. Unfortunately, her sixth child died from influenza at seven months old. Despite the personal trauma in her own life and a troubled marriage that deepened her depression, Eleanor supported her husband throughout his political career, served as his organizer and a key person in his political efforts. She walked alongside him through his roles as a New York State Senator, Assistant Secretary of the Navy, Governor of New York, and finally President of the United States.

Eleanor Roosevelt answered her calling to public service with each transition in Franklin's career and embraced the transformations occurring in the world in which she lived. Franklin Roosevelt became a New York State Senator at age 27 and moved his family to Albany. Eleanor Roosevelt played an essential role in the transition. Just before they arrived in Albany on January 1, 1911, she made preparations to have their home ready and planned an Open House for his supporters on Inaugural Day. After the event, she took the time to meet the neighbors in the area and promoted their political platform. While Franklin served as Assistant Secretary for the Navy in World War I, Eleanor committed her time and talents to the American Red Cross where she organized a canteen for the Navy Red Cross, knitted and distributed wool, and visited wounded sailors in the hospital.

Eleanor Roosevelt became an advocate for the progressive movement. She believed a person's environment played a critical role in the individual's social and political development. Eleanor was convinced that education was a sure way to enhance people's lives and lived out this belief by joining the campaign for women's rights. She became involved with the Internal Congress of Women's Workers. Ten years after the Washington, D.C. race riots of 1919, when 200 soldiers and sailors beat, lynched, and killed Black citizens in the streets, Eleanor Roosevelt fought to end segregation and discrimination and supported an anti-lynching law. Although the anti-lynching law never passed, she never gave up her desire to see a more just society.

Eleanor Roosevelt's political platform became more visible after her husband's unsuccessful run for Vice President of the United States in 1920. When Franklin fell ill with polio and became paralyzed, Eleanor Roosevelt became his public representative for political affairs. Members of the public and the Democratic Party began to notice her effectiveness and her respect as a public figure grew. Her growing political platform supported her work with the League of Women Voters and the Women's Trade Union League.

When Franklin Roosevelt won the presidential election in 1932, Eleanor's political career gained greater prominence and respect. She transformed the role of the United States First Lady from being solely a ceremonial hostess to one of advocacy and transformative leadership. Eleanor Roosevelt made her agenda visible to the American public from the Depression Years through World War II, when the American people were most divisive. She became a voice for the oppressed and those who were being held back and overlooked. She planned press conferences, developed radio broadcasts, and wrote a daily syndicated newspaper column to address personal, societal, and political issues. It was the first time that Americans witnessed a First Lady with such an extensive public speaking platform.

One way Eleanor Roosevelt accomplished her advocacy was to recommend certain minority leaders on committees that could bring about social change. One such example was President Roosevelt's appointment of Mary McLeod Bethune as Director of the Division of Negro Affairs of the National Youth Administration. Eleanor played an instrumental role in bringing attention to Bethune's qualification for the position. Thus, Mary McLeod Bethune became the first African American woman to head up a federal agency.

After her husband's death in 1945, Eleanor's role in civil rights, human rights, and political affairs expanded. She became a board member of the National Association for the Advancement of Colored

People (NAACP) in 1945. After accepting President Harry Truman's invitation to serve as a United Nations delegate sometime later, she became the chairperson for the United Nations Commission on Human Rights. She received acknowledgment of her work for her contribution to drafting the Universal Declaration of Human Rights. The document was adopted on December 10, 1948. Following more than two decades of service to the United Nations, Eleanor Roosevelt traveled to numerous foreign countries, accepted many speaking invitations, and continued her social justice and human rights advocacy until her death from tuberculosis in 1962.

Illustration depicting Eleanor Roosevelt holding
a poster of the Universal Declaration of Human Rights

4

Illustration depicting The Troubling Times The 1920s-1932, Roosevelt's New Deal, The World War II Years and the Decade Leading up to the Civil Rights Movement (1945-1955)

CHAPTER 4
The Times

"The First Lady of the Struggle" and "The First Lady of the World" grew up in two different socioeconomic and cultural systems in the same country. They generally interacted with people within their own social class and race. Their friendship began in 1927, ended with Bethune's death in 1955, and survived the difficult times, and significant societal change, including the economic crisis during the 1920s, the New Deal era, World War II, and the Pre-Civil Rights Movement.

The 1920s-1932

The "Roaring Twenties" was a time when the United States experienced significant growth. The country was rebuilding following the devastation of World War I. A manufacturing boom led Americans to move from farm areas throughout the country to cities. With technological advancements in communication, more Americans preferred to use radio rather than newspapers for information. In addition to technological advancements, one of the most notable social and political achievements was the acceptance of the 19th amendment by the United States Congress. This amendment guaranteed all American women the right to vote. However, this era of apparent stability and rising prosperity was short-lived.

Republican Herbert Hoover was inaugurated as the 31st President of the United States on March 4, 1929. But public optimism for his presidency quickly declined following the stock market collapse on

October 29, 1929. Since so many people had investments in the stock market, their investments became worthless when stock prices fell. What followed was The Great Depression, the most severe worldwide economic collapse. This ten-year crisis left the United States with record-high unemployment rates, deflation, and increased poverty.

Both Blacks and whites were dissatisfied with the state of U.S. affairs during the Depression. Blacks endured more discrimination, and lynchings increased at a rapid rate. There were also fewer opportunities for Blacks to advance themselves, and by 1932 approximately 50 percent of African Americans were unemployed. White families lost their status as companies in trouble began to lay off their employees. The slowdown in industrial production meant that more women lost their jobs. These were the women who had started working outside of the home during World War I.

Moreover, as the crash worsened, so did the struggle between Whites and Blacks and the fight to end the marginalization of women. Blacks received much lower wages than whites for the same job. Women were placed in powerless or unimportant positions. Despite these conditions, however, Roosevelt and Bethune became more powerful and influential.

Though they were not silent during those difficult years, the two women did not have frequent communication after their initial meeting in 1927. Faced with the pressures of securing financial support for her college, Bethune persisted amidst her frustrations about the limited support for Blacks and ventures to uplift them. The United

States was in a better financial position and was a major creditor to various countries throughout the world after World War I. However, women, Blacks, and children did not benefit from the wealth and financial stability the country was experiencing.

Bethune wrote to fellow school founder and Federation of Negro Women's Clubs member Charlotte Hawkins Brown to share her frustrations and strategies for keeping the college's doors open. She focused on enlisting new supporters and reaching out to old friends of her Daytona Beach school for donations to support the institution's operating budget.

In addition to promoting education and supporting their private schools, Bethune and Roosevelt became more intentional about empowering women. They believed combining women's collective efforts was a pathway to establishing a more stable and productive society. Bethune continued to lead and organize members of the National Association of Colored Women (NACW) during the early years of the Great Depression. She wanted the organization to go beyond addressing the struggles of black women to engage with women of other ethnicities. Bethune had a global vision. She wanted to unify NACW to address international challenges facing women of color, including those who were not African American. Simultaneously Roosevelt encouraged the women of the Junior League to fulfill certain expectations during the unemployment crisis. She urged them to think beyond their own interests as privileged white women and help create jobs for others in need.

The 1920s was also a time when racism in America took on a new form. During the first half of the decade, the Ku Klux Klan membership, which had declined during the Depression, began to increase. The organization suppressed Black voting through violence and intimidation. The National Association for the Advancement of Colored People (NAACP) vigorously attempted to use the legal system to eradicate or get rid of racist Jim Crow laws that enforced the segregation of Black Americans. These laws, which lasted from 1876 until 1965, made it illegal for Blacks to have the same privileges as Whites, particularly in public places, including access to water fountains and segregated restaurants, buses, schools, and restrooms.

As major corporations and financial institutions started failing during the 1930s, the Depression worsened, and the marginalization of women became more widespread. In 1931, the American Federation of Labor supported the discriminatory practice of not hiring women whose husbands received a reasonable wage. Further, the Economic Recovery Act of 1932 required women who the federal government employed to give up their positions to unemployed men. At that time, women's clubs strengthened their efforts to organize across the nation and address how marginalization affected families and their own well-being.

During the Hoover Administration, the Democratic Party used these unfavorable conditions to persuade voters to change party affiliation. In 1932, Franklin Delano Roosevelt won the presidential election by a landslide. As the 32nd President of the United States, he laid out a "new" contract he believed would restore the country's stability and

and power. Mary McLeod Bethune and Eleanor Roosevelt's relationship played a critical role in that "new" contract" and during FDR's presidency, their friendship began to have greater impact.

Roosevelt's New Deal

The "New Deal" involved several programs President Franklin Roosevelt created between 1933 and 1938 to address the aftermath of the Great Depression. He believed that the federal government could do more to help transition the country out of the economic and social distress resulting from the Depression. President Roosevelt held Congress for a special session that lasted 100 days.

During the "Hundred Days," Congress passed emergency relief programs, work relief programs, banking reform, as well as agricultural and farm legislation, including the Civilian Conservation Corps, Works Progress Administration, National Recovery Administration, Reconstruction Finance Corporation, Farm Credit Administration, Agricultural Adjustment Administration, and the Home Owners Loan Corporation. The newly created Federal Emergency Relief Administration received $500 million to help states support the needy. The Civil Works Administration (CWA) received authorization to provide employment for approximately 4 million people. Additionally, The Home Owners Loan Corporation worked with the government to evaluate mortgage foreclosures by adjusting mortgage terms of payment so more people would avoid losing their homes. The changes to the mortgage system provided the opportunity for more Americans to purchase homes if they had the minimum income to afford monthly payments.

Beyond the assistance given to help homeowners, President Roosevelt also extended programs to farmers facing bankruptcy. During the Depression years, farmers produced more food. But, many people were without jobs and did not have sufficient money to buy the goods. As part of the New Deal legislation, the Farm Credit Administration (FCA) provided aid to pay off the farmers' debts to prevent them from facing bankruptcy. The FCA also assisted in refinancing farm mortgages.

President Roosevelt's New Deal initiatives also helped ease some of the challenges women and African Americans faced with inequality. Eleanor Roosevelt recommended that her husband and his administration involve women in transforming the country by appointing them to key positions based on their expertise. Hence, there were several appointments and hiring of women and Blacks in influential, high-ranking positions at the federal level. Frances Perkins became the first woman to earn a cabinet appointment as Secretary of Labor. He appointed Marion Glass Banister as Assistant Treasurer, and Nellie Taylor Ross became U.S. Mint Director.

The prominent 1935 appointment of Bethune as Special Adviser to the President on Minority Affairs was encouraged by Eleanor Roosevelt. This role gave her greater access to the country's leadership and an opportunity to influence the national agenda. Moreover, Bethune assisted the Roosevelt administration in obtaining African Americans support for World War II. At first, she was hesitant to detach herself from the Republican Party. For many years, the Democratic Party had been known for supporting southern white supremacy. But, as Bethune became attracted to the policies of Franklin Delano Roosevelt, she insisted that Republicans were doing less for African Americans and used her growing public status and respect in the Black community to advocate for President Roosevelt's agenda. Consequently, she successfully convinced many African Americans to change their party affiliation from Republican to Democrat.

The World War II Years

When President Franklin Delano Roosevelt ran for a third term and won the election, he became the only United States President elected to a third presidential term. This historic election occurred during the second phase of the New Deal and coincided with America's entry into World War II. The War began in 1939 when notorious dictator and Germany's leader, Adolf Hitler, sent troops to invade Poland. Hitler's ultimate goal was to have Germany rule Europe. After the invasion of Poland, Britain and France launched a battle with Germany. This engagement marked the beginning of World War II. The United States entered the War on December 8, 1941, after the Japanese attacked the U.S. Naval Base at Pearl Harbor in Hawaii.

More than 50 nations participated in World War II. The United States prioritized its engagement in the War over its economic crisis. Millions of American men registered for the draft to defend America's position during the deadliest war in history. More than 2 million of them were Blacks. They defended America against its foreign adversaries while still fighting for the right to be recognized as citizens of the United

States who should be granted equal rights. The country's leading position in the War helped it earn the ranking as a superpower and leader of the "free world."

While American men defended the country's standing on the world stage, women entered the labor force in record numbers. Many assumed the role of breadwinners to support their families. They went from holding service and clerical positions to fulfilling jobs in factories and defense plants previously held by men. This change in women's roles was primarily because of the need to assist the war efforts from the home front. Although women earned more money during wartime than in earlier years, they still received far less pay than men who performed the same jobs.

Roosevelt and Bethune were among the women who actively employed their skills, talents, and influence to support the war efforts and the people impacted by the crisis at home and abroad. Roosevelt served as the Assistant Director of the Office of Civilian Defense. She supported the enlistment of civilians to assist in the war efforts. More than 350,000 women signed up to serve in the military during World War II. Some performed clerical roles and others worked as nurses, repaired aircrafts, and fought in active combat. As an honorary general of the Women's Army for National Defense (WAND), Bethune urged women to accept volunteer opportunities at home in connection with war efforts abroad. As Special Assistant to the Secretary of War for the Women's Army Auxiliary Corps, she helped increase the number of Black officers and encouraged people of color to give their best service to the war efforts.

Yet, Black women still faced significant challenges as the military remained segregated during most of World War II. Consequently, fewer defense jobs were available for them, and white women generally did not want to work alongside them. As racial tensions escalated throughout the country, Eleanor Roosevelt was frustrated that the government opposed racism abroad but did not prioritize its eradication at home. She urged the Roosevelt Administration to act urgently to end discrimination within the military and the defense industry.

Decade Leading up to the Civil Rights Movement (1945-1955)

Despite the unexpected death of President Franklin Roosevelt, in 1945, Bethune and Eleanor Roosevelt's friendship continued throughout the decade. It was ten years before the U.S. Civil Rights Movement began and only a few months before the Japanese surrendered at the end of World War II. America's victory in World War II was evident to the world. The country's financial conditions had improved, and the nation provided aid to foreign countries to help in their post-war recovery. Unemployment declined, and new industries developed products, like natural rubber, to accommodate military and civilian needs. The return of men from war to their homes led to the baby boom period. Young adults began marrying at an early age and created large families. And for the majority of Americans, it was a season of prosperity.

But with the benefits of the War, there were some disadvantages, misfortune, and setbacks. Positive changes in race relations fell short behind the improvements of other social issues. In general, white families began thriving again, but Black families did not. Segregation persisted. Blacks could not drink from the same water fountain or eat in the same restaurants as whites. Black and white children went to separate schools, and there was consistent opposition to the idea of school integration.

After President Roosevelt's sudden death in 1945, vice president, Harry S. Truman, assumed office as the 33rd President of the United States. Truman placed the issue of civil rights on the national agenda. He became the first President of the United States to address the National Association for the Advancement of Colored People (NAACP). Although Jim Crow laws remained active throughout the country, Truman strongly opposed prejudice and intolerance and called for eradicating discrimination in the United States.

During this decade, Bethune and Roosevelt continued their advocacy work on the home front. They asserted their positions about social conditions through their newspaper columns and public support of women's organizations and educational institutions. These women extended their efforts for equality and justice beyond American borders. Their travels throughout these years increased their prominence on the international stage as advocates for world peace. After World War II and before his death, FDR laid the groundwork for developing the United Nations (UN) as a global peacekeeping organization. Both Eleanor Roosevelt and Bethune contributed to the

UN's passage of the Universal Declaration of Human Rights. Eleanor Roosevelt chaired the commission that was responsible for drafting the document. Bethune was the only Black woman the State Department appointed as an associate consultant to the American delegation for the chartering of the UN. During Bethune's attendance at the 1945 State Conference, she suggested ideas to frame the organization's practices.

Years later, Black people persisted in the fight for equality. In 1954 the United States Supreme Court passed *Brown v. Board of Education*. This ruling supported the integration of children in schools and provided much-needed hope for a more just society. It concluded that segregated schools denied Black children equal opportunities for quality education. Another central turning point in the fight for justice was the Montgomery Bus Boycott that began with Rosa Parks' refusal to sit in the back of a bus in Montgomery, Alabama. The Boycott and the protests that followed increased the momentum of the American Civil Rights Movement.

Altogether the events of the 1920s, the New Deal era, World War II, and the Pre-Civil Rights Movement helped to mold the bond between Bethune and Eleanor Roosevelt. They advocated collectively and individually to make America a better place despite being surrounded by challenges.

5

Illustration depicting Eleanor Roosevelt meeting with Mary McLeod Bethune

CHAPTER 5
An Impactful Friendship

"My association with Eleanor Roosevelt has been one of the most enriching of my entire life. Our friendship has combined a deep, abiding understanding with a warm kinship that has been strengthened over the years"

(Bethune, 1949)

Mary McLeod Bethune was 52 years old, and Eleanor Roosevelt was 43 years old when Roosevelt's mother-in-law first introduced them in 1927. Mrs. James Roosevelt was hosting a luncheon, in New York, for leaders of women's organizations from around the country. As the only Black guest, Bethune received seating as an honored guest when it became clear the audience was uncomfortable by her presence. Though they did not immediately become friends, she and Eleanor made a connection after the luncheon and their unique kindred relationship evolved over nearly three decades.

At the time of their initial meeting, both women were fulfilling educational interests in different parts of the country. Bethune was leading the recently merged co-educational school in Daytona Beach, Florida. Similarly, Roosevelt was pursuing a teaching career at the Todhunter School in New York. They resumed communication in 1933, six years after their introduction. Although they had many private talks, their primary means of communication was through written letters. After their many years of association, a strong and important friendship developed.

The 1930s

The 1930s was a season of reconnecting and reestablishing the relationship. Initiated by a letter from Bethune to Roosevelt, on December 18, 1933, their reacquaintance occurred shortly after Roosevelt became First Lady of the United States. Bethune started most of the written communication during this period and made numerous requests for meetings with the First Lady. She requested Roosevelt to make public appearances as a show of support for various social groups and causes. Not long after their communication resumed, Bethune began working with the White House as a volunteer. By 1937 she was appointed to a full-time position with the National Youth Administration.

Both women recognized that their association and growing friendship was considered unpopular, but they chose to focus on how their highly visible partnership could improve racial conditions and enhance their reputations. Bethune positioned herself as a spokesperson for the Black community and was pleased with Eleanor and her husband's work through the New Deal program. Bethune wanted to ensure that the Roosevelt Administration did all it could to support the needs of Blacks, women, and youth. Consequently, she offered her insight into the Black community's struggles to Eleanor Roosevelt and encouraged the First Lady to share the information with President Roosevelt.

Through Bethune's insistence, Roosevelt encouraged her husband to consider Bethune's insights into supporting the Black communities. President Roosevelt took note of Bethune's influence in the Black community and appointed her as special adviser on minority affairs. She also became the first woman to lead his unofficial Black Cabinet, a presidential advisory council of all Black leaders.

The nature of the friendship during this decade was more political in nature. Many of their communications focused on government issues and how the Roosevelt Administration could improve the lives of Black Americans. However, as Bethune and Roosevelt collaborated to enhance the social conditions, their respect for each other and personal connection developed. They were able to identify the issues that were important to each other, and their collaboration around those common issues nurtured their personal bond. When the First Lady received verbal attacks because of her support for African Americans and particularly her relationship with Bethune, she ensured their association became more well-known. To that end, Roosevelt deliberately appeared in public with Bethune and escorted her by hand into the White House for meetings. Together, both women demonstrated immense courage under public scrutiny. They became more acutely aware of the advocacy needed to achieve both political and social change.

1940s

Roosevelt and Bethune gave more attention to their friendship during the 1940s. It was the decade in which they maintained the relationship and expanded their impact. They exchanged hundreds of letters proposing ways to use their influence to help each other achieve a specific outcome. When President Roosevelt died before taking office for the fourth term, the National Youth Administration was dissolved, and Bethune lost her full-time position. Yet, the friendship-building Bethune and Roosevelt engaged in during the previous decade set the stage for their deliberate, abiding, voluntary friendship to strengthen throughout this period.

Commonly called "the war years," this decade was complicated by the increase in lynchings and racial riots in the United States. These critical circumstances demanded their attention and required more united effort to further Roosevelt and Bethune's common agenda. The interactions in the 1940s demonstrated just how far Roosevelt was willing to go for a friend. They had more face-to-face meetings and telephone conversations, and their letters referred to what they discussed in those exchanges. Whether they sent written communication directly to each other or their secretaries sent correspondence on their behalf, the quality of their messages was straightforward and Bethune requested many personal favors. However, Bethune ensured her requests aligned with the issues Roosevelt cared about–education and the advancement of women. Consequently, Roosevelt became more engaged with Bethune's National Council of Negro Women and helped solicit funds for her Daytona Beach school.

Determined to promote equality locally and globally, both women embraced the opportunity to contribute to the transformative work of the United Nations. As a United States delegate, Roosevelt chaired the United Nations Commission on Human Rights and led it in drafting the Universal Declaration of Human Rights in 1948. Bethune was the only Black woman invited to the United Nations' founding conference and provided the United States delegation with advice and counsel. Roosevelt arranged for her involvement with the United Nations at Bethune's request. These two public figures were well-suited to contribute to this critical work since their interracial relationship had modeled the ideals of the UN – dignity, equal treatment, freedom, economic advancement, and educational opportunities for all human beings. Moreover, their friendship and combined political and social activism supported the principles incorporated into the Universal Declaration of Human Rights.

1950s

Following Roosevelt's White House years, she and Bethune had fewer face-to-face interactions and more infrequent communication. After President Roosevelt's death, Eleanor returned to Hyde Park, New York. Nonetheless, she regularly returned to the nation's capital for meetings with leaders and as part of her appointment to the Human Rights Commission of the United Nations. Bethune remained in Washington, DC for some time during the 1940s to oversee the operations for the National Council of Negro Women. However, by 1950 she had returned to Daytona Beach, FL and retired for the second time as President of Bethune-Cookman College. Although their interactions decreased and the focus of their friendship shifted, what did not weaken was their desire to maintain the relationship.

Separated by distance, Roosevelt and Bethune often expressed how much they missed each other. Both women had gotten older, their schedules had dramatically slowed down, and they wrote fewer letters.

However, more telegrams were sent to check on each other's well-being. In 1950, Bethune wrote to Roosevelt, "I hope you have had a marvelous trip and are refreshed in mind and body. Always know that wherever you are – on land or on sea – my prayers are with you and for you."

The correspondences they exchanged during these years conveyed their admiration for each other and their willingness to support each other's efforts. At another time in 1950, when Bethune-Cookman College commemorated the founder's 75th birthday, Roosevelt could not attend, but sent a note expressing joy in joining Bethune's friends in celebrating her. "You have had a very useful life. I send my caring and best wishes for the future." When Roosevelt turned 66 in October of that year, Bethune sent a special note without her usual personal requests. "God has been marvelously good to all of us in permitting you to live, grow, and serve during these years... My prayers are that strength and courage and increasing wisdom may be yours as the years go by..."

Bethune continued to encourage the former First Lady to make special appearances for Black colleges and interracial causes and maintain their friendship despite geographic separation. Roosevelt's involvement with the United Nations absorbed much of her time, and she could not accommodate all of Bethune's requests. Yet, she made every effort to solicit funding for Bethune's institution.

Organizational Impact and Involvement

Bethune and Roosevelt supported several organizations including The Women's Army Auxiliary Corps and the National Association for the Advancement of Colored People. They contributed to the establishment and development of organizations as they represented their personal beliefs about social and political affairs. However, they mainly corresponded about three organizations: the National Youth Administration (NYA), Bethune-Cookman College (B-CC), and the National Council of Negro Women (NCNW). Accordingly, their collaborative work on behalf of these organizations reflected the impact of their friendship.

Roosevelt has been hailed as the mastermind behind the creation of the NYA, the agency formed to address the needs of underserved youth. Following the Great Depression, the agency targeted its efforts to support minorities. Bethune was the pioneer who founded the Historical Black Bethune-Cookman College, which later became an accredited college for Blacks. When Bethune elected to create an organization for women in support of interracial advancement, Roosevelt was one of the first women to support her vision.

NYA

Roosevelt believed involving minorities in FDR's New Deal initiatives would strengthen the Administration's recovery response and ensure that minorities were included in the planned programming. Bethune's involvement was inspired and encouraged by Eleanor Roosevelt. President Roosevelt offered Bethune a permanent position with the agency shortly after she accepted a volunteer position as a member of the National Youth Administration's National Advisory Committee.

In 1936, Bethune delivered her assessment of the NYA's efforts with minorities to President Roosevelt and the NYA Executive Committee. She compelled the agency to continue providing supplemental funds to help impoverished southern Blacks whom she said respected the NYA's efforts to help minorities support their children's medical expenses, school supplies, and social activities. President Roosevelt created the NYA's Office of Minority Affairs and appointed her to lead the new division in response to her convincing presentation.

However, Bethune rarely directly lobbied the President or agency heads, but usually directed her advocacy to her friend. She encouraged Roosevelt to use her influence to accomplish specific legislative or executive decisions. As Minority Affairs Director for the NYA, Bethune often recommended qualified Blacks to the First Lady for administrative positions with the federal government. In 1941, she recommended twenty-five qualified Black women for paid or volunteer federal government positions. Despite their inability to meet many of Bethune's desires, both President Roosevelt and the First Lady valued her judgment and seriously considered her recommendations.

At one point, in 1941, Bethune petitioned for help in facilitating expansion of a Negro hospital in Wilmington, North Carolina, by imploring that,

> They have a little community of 35,000 people, and Uncle Sam placed in their midst two Army camps with facilities for 35,000 soldiers and a large shipyard for the construction of thirty-seven

> 10,000 ton steel freighters. This influx of Negro defense workers has so flooded the existing hospital facilities that it is fundamental that federal aid be immediately given to relieve this condition...We know Mrs. Roosevelt how interested you are in all of these affairs so I am bringing this pressing problem to you for special consideration. This matter is now pending in the Federal Works Agency and I am asking you to take a moment and see to it that this one project is brought to the attention of the proper persons with your personal emphasis...

Roosevelt acted promptly to respond to Bethune's request through the NYA. Her secretary replied three days after Bethune's September 26, 1941 letter. She indicated that Roosevelt requested the Federal Works Agency to expedite their work. The Federal Works Agency acknowledged they were facing challenges with the Office of Public Health and told Roosevelt they were "...making every effort to expedite the project you now have under consideration."

On another occasion, when Bethune informed Roosevelt about racial discrimination toward defense workers, the First Lady promptly escalated the concern to the President's office, and President Roosevelt signed Executive Order 8802, prohibiting discrimination within defense industries. Bethune was particularly grateful for Eleanor Roosevelt's favorable assistance. She wrote,

> We can never express our appreciation to you for your interest in the whole affair and the signing of the Executive Order by our President on June 25. Not since Abraham Lincoln spoke

> on that memorable day of the emancipation of slaves has such a far reaching Executive Order come forth for the benefit of my people...In my own weak way I am standing on the sidelines trying to help to direct the emphasis of thought and action in the right direction. I want you to feel that you can always depend upon me and if there is any suggestion or consultation I can give please let me know.

At the end of the letter, Bethune recommended Earl Dickerson for membership on the five-man Presidential Board to investigate racial discrimination in the defense industries. Importantly, Dickerson was a civil rights lawyer and activist. Roosevelt assured Bethune she would send her recommendation to President Roosevelt and Dickerson was eventually appointed.

Bethune-Cookman College

Roosevelt and Bethune shared a common interest in the education of youth. Having spent several years in the classroom, Roosevelt did not want to see people denied their right to education because of discriminatory laws and practices. She said, "One of the best ways of enslaving a people is to keep them from education and thus make it impossible for them to understand what is going on in the world as a whole." Similarly, Bethune felt marginalized minorities could obtain liberation if they received a meaningful education.

Bethune's commitment to preserve and sustain the institution she founded with only $1.50, five little girls, and faith in God, was quite pronounced during her 28-year friendship with Eleanor Roosevelt. Bethune kept the institution at the forefront of the First Lady's mind through a significant exchange of correspondences. She noted the academic achievements of its students, matters of institutional growth, and the financial needs. Their relationship helped increase public awareness of the College, attracted new donors, benefactors, government aid, and positioned it as a creditable institution of higher learning.

Shortly after Bethune reconnected with Roosevelt in 1933, Bethune started inviting her to visit the College. Roosevelt respectfully declined quite a number of those invitations until 1939. That year, she attended the College's 35th Anniversary celebration. By this time, Bethune had begun her official position as Director of the Division of Negro Affairs for the NYA. As their camaraderie strengthened and Bethune's public profile moved to the national stage, Roosevelt offered more support paying three additional visits to Bethune–Cookman in 1940, 1943, and 1953. The media paid attention to her visits to a Negro College and she purposedly disclosed the nature of her visits to the nationwide audience of her daily syndicated "My Day" columns published six days a week.

Roosevelt used her February 20, 1940 column to highlight her first formal visit to Bethune's school:

> It was surprising to me how many representatives there were from other schools and colleges to bring Mrs. Bethune congratulations on her work and good wishes for the future...

> Until I went over the plant, I never realized what a really dramatic achievement this junior College is. It ministers to the needs of 100,000 Negroes from Daytona south, and it takes 250 students. The object is to train leaders who will return to their communities and serve their people in whatever line of activity they have chosen as a life work. Thirty-five years ago, Mrs. Bethune began with five little girls. The first land was bought with the first five dollars earned. This land up to that time had been part of the city dump in a portion of the city known as "Hell's Hole."

Roosevelt served as an unofficial ambassador to the College, educating the broader American society about its history and importance. She not only promoted the institution but appealed to her readers to give their support. She wrote,

> Like all other colleges, they still need a great deal—a library building, for instance, and many more books. From this small library in Bethune-Cookman College, books are sent travelling around into the various rural districts of the vicinity. They need a substantial endowment fund, a building where better shop work can be done, for at present the quarters are too small. Somehow, I have a feeling that this work is going to grow and that Mrs. Bethune's dream is going to carry her people far along the way to better education and better standards of living.

Bethune valued that support and acknowledged her efforts. Her note to Roosevelt read,

> Your visit to us was glorious. It was the supreme moment in the life of Bethune-Cookman College. May we thank you. The story you sent out to the world through your column will be an everlasting blessing.

Following her visit to Bethune-Cookman College in 1953, Roosevelt brought attention to the advancements made in improving race relations in the South. She was pleasantly surprised at the number of people who attended the reception at the College. The impact of her presence earned positive attention for the school. It was Roosevelt's last visit as Bethune died two years later.

Roosevelt fully supported the institution's financial stability. Although she did not make many personal monetary contributions, particularly in the 1930s, she lent her support to meet some of the needs of the College. In 1941 she agreed to serve on the College's Board of Trustees, and in 1942 endorsed the institution's Endowment Campaign by agreeing to serve as Honorary Chairman of the Committee to help raise $1,137,000. She petitioned many individual donors for the College and requested that some of the honorariums from various speaking engagements be earmarked to Bethune-Cookman instead. After leaving the White House, she occasionally made personal pledges and contributions in her own name.

Roosevelt understood that the College would continue to receive the public's support if she remained affiliated. But more importantly, she wanted to support the vision of her friend. When Bethune retired and Roosevelt wanted to step down from the Board, she remained at Bethune's request though she could no longer attend meetings.

In 1949, Roosevelt continued to hold her position as Honorary Chair of the national campaign to increase the College's endowment. In a photograph with Bethune, included in a 25-page campaign pamphlet, the caption above the picture read, "A long-time friend–Mrs. Eleanor Roosevelt–leads a national campaign sponsored by many distinguished Americans. The College seeks support from a number of sources." The campaign press release featured quotes approved by Eleanor Roosevelt. She said,

> Bethune-Cookman College has been making a positive contribution to our democracy in the higher education of Negro youth...If, however, its service is to keep pace with the demands now being placed upon it, the College must have greatly expanded facilities.

Roosevelt's endorsements, College visits, and media coverage resulted in overwhelming donor support for the institution. Her joint efforts with Bethune improved the institution's credibility and garnered the trust needed to get the attention of benefactors. Some of Roosevelt's most important friends demonstrated their support with individual donations. Among them were Mrs. Henry Pfeiffer who donated $12,500 and Mary Woodward Lasker who gave $1000. Lasker's follow up letter noted,

> My husband and I are very much interested in what Mrs. Bethune had to say about the work of her College...We strongly agree with you that the negro problem is of great importance, and would like to help....we do not feel that we can make any contribution to the endowment but are enclosing this check to help defray the current expenses of the College.

Roosevelt believed in Bethune's vision and shared her passion for educating Blacks. For this reason, she helped to seek new donors and nurtured existing donors she had introduced to the College. Despite criticism from political associates, she was determined to help Bethune keep the doors of the institution open.

National Council of Negro Women

Much like the work they did for Bethune-Cookman and the National Youth Administration, Roosevelt and Bethune mutually supported the mission of the National Council of Negro Women. Their friendship reflected the interracial cooperation among women that the NCNW desired to promote and achieve.

Roosevelt used her "My Day" columns to strategically promote the organization's work founded by her friend. In her December 20, 1937 article, she reported, "I dressed a Christmas tree in the afternoon at the Women's Trade Union League; spoke for Mrs. Bethune at her meeting of the National Council of Negro Women, and motored up to Hyde Park." At times she used the lead sentence in an article to support the women's group. On October 28, 1940, the lead read, "Friday afternoon, at the White House, I received the National Council of Negro Women, who are holding their convention in the District of Columbia." Eleanor Roosevelt enthusiastically engaged nationwide support for NCNW's role in encouraging the armed forces. She knew Americans held deeply rooted sentiments and admiration for the military and would pay closer attention to NCNW as an organization for racial uplift.

Some of the accomplishments of the NCNW were a direct result of Bethune and Eleanor Roosevelt's relationship. Roosevelt arranged the 1938 meeting of 65 of the organization's members with the Department of the Interior and various other government officials. This gathering allowed them to discuss their plans to help Black women obtain government jobs.

NCNW proposed that inclusion of more people of color would lead to more significant consideration of Black problems. Determining the matter needed further discussion, Roosevelt arranged a meeting at the White House with government officials from various agencies and the NCNW committee. At this session, Bethune recommended qualified Black women to serve in leadership positions at government agencies such as the Women's Bureau of the Labor Department, the Social Security Board, and the Children's Bureau.

The First Lady helped the National Council of Negro Women expand its agenda. On the Council's tenth anniversary in 1945, Roosevelt provided strategies she believed would improve their operations. According to the minutes from the March 24, 1945 meeting,

> Mrs. Roosevelt stated that the National group should be gathering information from all its constituents, and then someone at the national level analyze the reports of the local groups. National contacts are where things get started. It is there that these reports should be compiled and passed on to local groups. Make contacts with national and international groups.

Further, Roosevelt highlighted how she and the President's Administration continued to involve the minority perspective in various social issues on the national agenda. Her support of Bethune's organization reflected the common interests she shared with her and the strength of the friendship which, according to civil rights activist and mutual friend, Dr. Dorothy Height, "never waned; [and] was ever stronger."

The Close Friendship

Bethune and Roosevelt were not intimidated by each other's differences, the unwelcoming social or political climate, nor their own fears. They intentionally allowed their relationship to evolve from formal to political to personal. They were focused on the positive outcomes that their relationship could achieve for the society in which they lived.

Classism, racism, and public criticism could have kept them apart. Yet, these were the difficult situations that united them. As innovators and solutions seekers, Bethune and Roosevelt were determined to bring people together amidst their differences. Their friendship succeeded because they combined their unique perspectives with a shared vision, aspirations, and ideals that strengthened their bond.

Successful friendships involve mutual support. For Roosevelt and Bethune, support was selfless. They were kind and respectful to each other, showed compassion in sickness, offered prayers at times of distress, and wished each other well. They focused their friendship on building relational, economic, educational, political, and social bridges to improve people's lives. Theirs was a political friendship and a close friendship that evolved over nearly three decades. It was unique, intentional, impactful, and unusual.

Illustration depicting meeting with Dorothy Height, Eleanor Roosevelt and Mary McLeod Bethune

Illustration depicting Eleanor Roose
Mary McLeod Bethune holding a scro
"A Call for Civility"

6

CHAPTER 6
A Call for Civility

Despite lingering elements of racism, inequality, and discrimination in our society, the relationship between Mary McLeod Bethune and Eleanor Roosevelt still serves as a model for achieving social progress. Their relationship promoted civility–respectful interaction and regard for others. Bethune and Roosevelt's association served as a type of social bridge. Through their connection, they were able to approach conflicts and inequalities that had long been unresolved within American society.

For Eleanor Roosevelt and Mary McLeod Bethune, civility was not simply a political device; it was the foundation of their communication and collaborative work. They desired to create national and global impact, and adopted a posture of civility in advocating for educational equality, politics, racial equality, women's empowerment, and human rights.

As 20th Century innovators and thought leaders, Mary McLeod Bethune and Eleanor Roosevelt's style of leadership and perspectives on interracial cooperation were uncommon. They shared their views with honesty and respect, and their communication focused on an outcome that would be mutually beneficial to improve society.

Roosevelt and Bethune's unusual friendship during such extraordinary times demonstrated how civility can improve the community. Its impact and influence confirmed the importance of engaging in intentionally respectful, intelligent, honest, and compassionate communication to change the existing political and social situations. It also produced a new normal for cross-racial, multidimensional female friendships regardless of the historical context.

Let us engage in the uncommon acts of service as Mary McLeod Bethune and Eleanor Roosevelt modeled through their friendship.

A Pledge to Civility as a Citizen of the World (Inspired by the impactful friendship between Eleanor Roosevelt & Mary McLeod Bethune)

As a "Citizen of the World," I ____________________, believe all humanity is connected despite differences in gender, race, color, ethnicity, politics, religion, education, and culture.

I believe civility begins with me and is a way to protect my rights and the rights of others to "life, liberty, and the pursuit of happiness."

I recognize that poverty, injustice, and discrimination will always exist, but civility is the antidote for a more enriched, impartial society.

To help people of the world advance and minimize the effects of past, present, and future harm caused by uncivil acts of humanity, **I seek to uphold the model of civility Eleanor Roosevelt and Mary McLeod Bethune embodied before the world.**

Therefore,

I pledge to respect myself and respectfully communicate with others regardless of age, ethnic, religious, political, gender, cultural, or social differences.

I pledge to maintain high ethical standards, communicate honestly and take full responsibility for my own actions.

I pledge to seek solutions to problems and contribute to building bridges that advance humanity instead of creating walls that create global division and conflict.

I pledge to promote civility every day through my actions and my words and intentionally honor the legacy of Mary McLeod Bethune and Eleanor Roosevelt.

____

Signature **Date**

BIBLIOGRAPHY

Bethune, M.M. (1942). What are we fighting for? In A. T. McCluskey & E. M. Smith (Eds.) (1999), *Mary McLeod Bethune: Building a better world, essays and selected documents (pp. 246-247).*

Bethune, M.M. (1949). I knew Franklin D. Roosevelt. Mary McLeod Bethune Papers: The Bethune-Cookman College Collection, 1922-1955. Carl Swisher Library, Bethune-Cookman University, Daytona Beach, Florida.

Bethune, M. M. (1955, August). My last will and testament. *Ebony*, 10, 105-110.

Flemming, S. Y. (1995). *The answered prayer to a dream: Bethune-Cookman College 1904-1994.* Virginia Beach, VA: Donning.

Frederick, H. (2000, February 10). Stay the course. Daytona Beach News Journal, Neighbors C1, C4.

Granger, D. (2002). Friendships Between Black and White Women. *American Behavioral Scientist*, 45, 1208-1213.

Height, D. I. (2003). *Open wide the freedom gates: A memoir.* New York, NY: Public Affairs.

Lash, J. (1972). *Eleanor: The years alone.* New York, NY: W. W. Norton & Company, Inc.

Leonard, R., & Locke, D.C. (1993). Communication stereotypes: Is interracial communication possible? *Journal of Black Studies, 23,* 332-343.

Manzueta, C. S. C. (2011). *Eleanor Roosevelt and Mary McLeod Bethune: An unusual friendship during uncommon times and its continued contribution to social change.* (Publication No. 3448298) [Doctoral dissertation, Regent University]. ProQuest Dissertations and Theses Global.

Martin, E. D. (2004). Mary McLeod Bethune: *Matriarch of black America*. Philadelphia, PA: Xlibris Corporation.

McCluskey, A. T. & Smith, E. M. (1999). *Mary McLeod Bethune: Building a better world, essays and selected documents.* Bloomington, IN: Indiana University Press.

McElvaine, R. S. (1993). *The Great Depression: America, 1929-1941.* New York, NY: Three Rivers Press.

Nash, G. D. (1992). *The crucial era: The Great Depression and World War II 1929-1945*. New York, NY: St. Martin Press.

Roosevelt, E. (1930). Good citizenship: The purpose of education. *Pictorial Review, 31*, 4, 94 & 97.

Roosevelt, E. (1953, February). Some of my best friends are Negro. *Ebony*, 9, 16-20, 22, 24-26.

Roosevelt, E. (1989). *Eleanor Roosevelt's My Day: Her Acclaimed Columns*, 1936-1945 (Vol. 1). Pharos Books.

Steinhorn, L., & Diggs-Brown, B. (2000). *By the color of our skin: The illusion of integration and the reality*. New York: Plume.

NOTES

Chapter 5 - Personal Communication

E. Roosevelt, personal communication, n.d.

M. M. Bethune, personal communication, July 1, 1950.

M. M. Bethune, personal communication, October 12, 1950.

M. M. Bethune, personal communication, September 26, 1941.

J. Carmody, personal communication, October 8, 1941.

M.M. Bethune, personal communication, July 10, 1941.

M.M. Bethune, personal communication, February 24, 1940.

W.H.A. Carr, personal communication, October 5, 1949.

R. Stephens, personal communication, September 19, 1949.

M. Lasker, personal communication, May 19, 1942.

NCNW Minutes of Conference, personal communication, March 24, 1945.

D. Height, personal communication, July 9, 2008.

Illustration depicting Eleanor Roosevelt presenting Mary McLeod Bethune with an honorary doctorate

Made in the USA
Las Vegas, NV
02 December 2023